Pay Attention to the Obvious

There's No Mystery to Great Leadership

By Eric Shaffer

Introduction

Many answers to the challenges we face in life and at work are pretty obvious, yet we often don't see them there in front of us jumping up and down and waving their arms for attention. Like our minds during a magician's illusion of disappearance, we miss the obvious explanation because we already believe in a mysterious or unexplained answer. It's the same with business. We often think the answer lies 'out there' beyond ourselves and the organization.

Life is just not that mysterious. Star athletes are star athletes because they have natural talent, drive and practice more than others. People will lose weight if they eat less. A sales force will thrive when it practices the principles employed by great sales forces.

But sometimes leaders can't see the forest through the trees, losing themselves in the details (trees) and forgetting the larger picture or vision (forest). Take heart, however, because you are not alone if this happens to you from time to time.

*****

I was working as a Director of Managed Markets for a medical device company which was facing a patient affordability issue. The medical device was often covered by insurance, but if it was not, the patient had to pay several hundred dollars, which was a financial hardship for most. And this wasn't a new problem. The medical device had been around for several years and a competitor had the same issue.

I had my Epiphany of the Obvious while talking to a physician about the device, his patients and the insurance coverage. He confirmed my idea that thought more patients would use our device if we allowed them to make 12 monthly payments. Talk about obvious! Yet none of us had thought of it before then.

Of course, executing the program was not so simple. It required a lot of strategy, analysis, and marketing. But for a year we had an advantage over our competition — until they copied our payment program.

*****

What I've set out to do here is bring the good—and not so good—elements of leadership to life with real-world examples to help you learn, grow and evolve as an effective, successful leader. The book gives you a short and precise summary of some of the critical keys to great leadership—many of which are right under our noses.

This book comes from many years working with a variety of high level leaders, as well as my own experience building and leading teams in leadership, management, managed markets, business, sales, communication, and Lean Six Sigma.

You will notice that I sometimes discuss leadership and management in the same sentence. Leaders are visionary, strategic, identify their team's strengths, develop, inspire, and lead teams to execute and achieve remarkable results. Managers are tacticians and make sure their teams are following objectives and goals. Those who are truly great are excellent at both and alternate between the two roles.

The essence of this book is to be short and to-the-point without a lot of bravado. Imagine that this is a friendly conversation between you and me. I want this to be a good use of your time with the hope that you can take away something to help you and your company soar to new heights.

Key #1 Do the Right Thing

" *I hate his kind. They use their integrity and hard work to advance their careers.* "

So what do I mean by "doing the right thing?" It seems to be an ambiguous statement; it could mean many things. Do I mean you should be honest? Well, yes that is important. It would make sense that if you want to be a leader you must tell the truth.

Honesty generally means that whatever you've done, good or bad, you speak the truth about it. This is definitely a good quality to possess, and you do want your team to know you are honest. However, "doing the right thing" is deeper than just honesty, it is about integrity and strength of character.

Integrity means that you adhere to a moral conviction, or code of honor, that won't allow you to do certain things that you feel would debase you or others. Someone who has integrity chooses to do the right thing when nobody is watching. Integrity builds trust.

Think of it this way. I am sure that your neighbor or neighbors are very nice people and that you probably are very polite and pleasant to each other. You may share tools, good conversation and sometimes enjoy dinner together. Now let us pretend there is a countrywide famine. Food and clean drinking water are scarce. Your family is hungry and thirsty and one or more may perish. Do you think there would continue to be a collegial relationship with your neighbors, or do you think there might be competition of survival of the fittest? Would your neighbor be a source of comfort and help, or a bitter adversary plotting how to take the food you and your family so desperately need?

In this example, there is an opportunity for you and your neighbor to show integrity by working together for the good of each other even in difficult and life threatening times. Values and integrity in times of great hardship are not compromised, but are practiced. This is the time when what we say we are as human beings becomes more than words, but actions. Those actions, if noble and true, are integrity.

In times of crisis such as a famine, there are three paths an individual can take.

1. Isolate to hide or provide protection from intruders. Maybe they have a bunker or a hidden room they can hide in until the threat is over.

2. Attack and take what one needs to survive from those that are weaker. Expose and use the weakness of adversaries to exploit and trap them to take what they have.

3. Unite and help those who want to work together to synergize talents, skills and staples for the group, team or community to survive and one day thrive. Lead with strength and conviction to help and defend the team. It may even mean self-sacrifice for the good of the group.

Today, we are in a jobs famine. There is no better time to see examples in the workplace of true integrity. How are individuals in your workplace acting as their future is threatened? Which of the three paths are they taking as they go through the challenge of one of the worst employment situations since the Great Depression? Which path are you on? The sustainability and long term success of companies will require that leaders have integrity, honesty and character.

> "Integrity is doing the right thing when no one is there to hear it, see it or give you credit for it." ~ Teresa M. Shaffer, Certified Executive Coach

> "No man can tell whether he is rich or poor by turning to his ledger. It is the heart that makes a man rich. He is rich according to what he is, not according to what he has." ~ Henry Ward Beecher

> "Integrity is not a conditional word. It doesn't blow in the wind or change with the weather. It is your inner image of yourself, and if you look in there and see a man who won't cheat, then you know he never will." ~John D. MacDonald

"Integrity includes the courage to do the right thing – even when it is hard. A person has Integrity when there is no gap between intent and behavior.....when he or she is whole, seamless, the same inside and out. This is congruency which will ultimately create credibility and trust."

~ Stephen M.R. Covey, *The Speed of Trust*

Until you know your strengths and weaknesses, you will always be your own roadblock or constraint. Do I mean you need to go through endless assessments and read countless introspective books? No, I don't. But you must realize there are things you are good at and things you are not, and you need to know what those are. You must be self-aware.

We all have a picture in our mind of what we look like, how we sound, and how we are perceived. However, sometimes that picture can be inaccurate. Some individuals can't step away and look at themselves realistically. An example would be a beautiful girl looking in the mirror and seeing herself as ugly. On the other side of the spectrum, someone who has an over-inflated sense of themselves will believe that they are never wrong and their way is always correct.

Have you ever said any of the following to yourself? *I take terrible pictures. When I see myself on camera, I look different. I look fat. I didn't notice that bald spot! I look old.* Well, the camera doesn't lie. Sure, a good photographer can use filters or airbrush flaws, but in general, what you see in a picture is pretty much how you look. You must keep in mind you have filters, as do other people. So your perception or filter of yourself can alter how you think you look. The same goes for the filters others see you through.

A few years ago I took on the challenge to add crown molding and wainscoting to my dining room. When I was finished it did look great, but I knew where every flaw was located. Every time I entered the room my eyes were drawn to the imperfections.

Jim, one of my good friends and also an amateur woodworker came to my house to see what I had done. He was very impressed and complimented me on the attention to detail and how it looked like a professional had remodeled my dining room.

I was very thankful for Jim's praise, but told him there were a few imperfections that I wasn't too happy about. I showed him the flaws and his reaction to them made me feel much better. Jim said, "If you didn't show me the flaws I would have never seen them. Even though I know they are there, it doesn't take anything away from what you did. The room is incredible." After that, when I walked into the dining room, I stopped focusing on the imperfections, and I began to appreciate a job well done. My perception or "filter" had changed.

The Importance of Constructive Feedback

So how do you learn how others' perceive you? There are several ways to learn about you on different dimensions. I would suggest you take assessments such as Strength Finders, the Myers-Briggs Type Indicator (MBTI) and Emotional Intelligence Test.

Other great feedback is from your manager. What are they seeing?

Have you ever noticed after most people get feedback on ways to improve from their supervisor, they disagree with their perceptions? They will go home and complain to their spouse that their boss doesn't know what they are talking about. "How can they say I need to improve in strategic thinking and planning or collaborating across boundaries? I'm great at these competencies." Well, the supervisor was probably right and committed to the direct report's growth and development. And if other individuals bring up the same issue, then it is probably an accurate assessment.

360 feedback from subordinates is valuable, but it is possible for a less than stellar supervisor to be given high marks for leadership because they lead by fear. I've also observed very talented leaders get lower marks because they were holding subordinates accountable and raising the bar for performance. Feedback from someone that has an ulterior motive other than your development should be looked at judiciously and should be vetted with other feedback from your peers, manager and stakeholders. More often than not, 360 assessments are a great complimentary tool to develop competencies and leaders in a company.

One of the best ways to see your strengths or weakness is on video. If you are practicing an upcoming presentation for a sales meeting or coaching an individual, it's a great way to give you some insights on how you could be perceived. Videotaping a team meeting can give you insight into how you communicate with your team and the body language of a group as well as their attentiveness to your message and influence. You can view how your message was perceived as well as your delivery. When you watch your video, you can assess if you are able to keep your own attention. Do you find yourself drifting off instead of paying attention to your own video? In other words, are you boring or engaging and inspiring the people in the meeting?

The Truth Can Hurt

One of the best training tools I ever participated in was during a management training class. A group of eight new managers was given the task of deciding what they would do if they were all in a plane that went down in a desert. The scenario played out that the radio and transponder were broken. The team members were given a list of items — blankets, food, plastic sheets, etc. — that we had to all agree to keep or discard. We also had to decide if we would stay with the plane or risk it and traipse across the desert to find help.

The entire process was videotaped and we had an audience of senior executive leadership. It was a good learning tool on teams and utilizing other's knowledge, abilities, and skills, but it also showed how we interacted with the group. Imagine eight new managers role-playing in front of senior leadership. Eight new managers trying to show each other up and prove to the senior leaders who were the best. It was like throwing eight young roosters in a small pen and letting them fight it out until only the alpha rooster remained.

After the demonstration of inexperience, we sat down to watch the video. I actually thought it was going to show me as one of the top leaders. As we all watched the video, I became disenchanted with my performance, as did the other young managers. The video showed our lack of listening and suboptimal team decision making skills. I was embarrassed how I interacted and conveyed my opinions. The video threw cold water on my delusions of grandeur.

The trainer in charge asked what we learned from the videotape. After the group discussed and critiqued our performance, it concluded:

1. We lacked the insight to see the benefit others could bring to the group and we ignored other group members' strengths.
2. We thought we performed well, but after we observed the videotape, realized our self perceptions and self-awareness wasn't accurate.
3. We had a few leadership competencies to develop like setting strategy and influencing for the greater good.

We were not self-aware of our strengths and weaknesses. Our lack of awareness blocked our ability to recognize the strengths of others that would have cancelled out our weaknesses so we could move forward as a unified and strong team.

Knowing yourself, self-awareness, your strengths, and your weaknesses are important to developing into a strong leader. You need to understand how you are perceived and how you communicate. If you are going to build a team, you want to compliment your strengths with your team's strengths. And don't be too hard on yourself. Everyone has unique strengths and weaknesses. You can compile the assessments and have your boss, a human resource colleague or an executive coach help you build a development plan to continuously improve.

Key #3 Be Emotionally Aware

Dr. Spotnuck was beloved by his patients for his caring bedside manner.

What is emotional awareness? A high-level overview of emotional awareness is the ability to put oneself in someone else's shoes. It is the ability to communicate not only with confidence and influence but also with empathy and humility. It is the understanding that you aren't perfect and are fallible. It is also letting others be fallible, so they can learn and grow from their mistakes. It is the understanding that you aren't always right and everyone else isn't always wrong — that there is more than one way to achieve a goal or an objective and there is more than one leadership style that works. In fact, there are many ways to achieve a desired goal or objective and there are many great leaders with different styles.

Emotional awareness requires maturity, vision beyond your own needs, and the ability to see the larger picture. It means having an understanding that not all answers are easy, and there may be sacrifices and delays on the road to achieving long-term goals.

It is very important that you put yourself in another's shoes to understand where they are coming from. You need to understand what stressors they have, what is worrying them and keeping them up at night. You also need to understand what motivates and inspires others to take action and pursue excellence.

When communicating with one or with many, you need to choose your words carefully. Put yourself in the audience's shoes and think how you would react to your message. Emotional awareness is not only your awareness, but understanding your audience's emotional awareness.

I will stress, when you are communicating via email, voice mail, WebEx, or a live presentation, understanding your audience is extremely important. Your words will be weighed very carefully and will be analyzed and dissected by the audience. Although you think your presentation is over when you are no longer talking, it will continue to be evaluated, analyzed and discussed for hours to days later. And if you are not careful, and you say something that could be construed as negative, even though you had no intent to say it in a negative way, it will be caught by many in the audience. It will be the focus of what was remembered about your presentation.

Emotional Unawareness Will Live on in Infamy

At a national sales meeting, a vice president was talking about how well the sales force had done meeting their yearly goals. In fact they had done so well that the VP was announcing improvements to their health plan and 401K benefits. Then he announced that the company car choices had been enhanced to include SUVs. There was a loud cheer from the sales force. Most of the sales representatives stood up to clap and many were pumping their fists in excitement.

Then the VP said that if a sales representative wanted a SUV, the added cost would be subtracted from their weekly paycheck.

The room immediately went quiet followed by the hum of a thousand whispers of disappointment. After the VP was finished speaking, his comments lived on in hours of negative conversations. There were no discussions about the improvements to the 401K plan or health plan, only negative comments about the company car plan.

Now there are two lessons to be learned here. First, the VP should have carefully weighed his words on how he presented the change to company car choices. He tried to spin it as a huge benefit for the employees when it really was not an improvement at all. He should have used some emotional awareness before he presented the change. He may have been better off having the Fleet Department issue a memo to the sales force that a cost to the employee would be added if they want an SUV as a company car.

The second lesson is the reaction from the sales force. Yes, the change in company car options could have been worded differently, but many of the sales representatives ignored all the good news and just focused on what they observed as a negative. People inherently look for the negative. If there were 100 positives and one negative, there are many people that will focus on the one negative.

Use Emotional Awareness with Both Your Manager and Direct Reports

Using emotional awareness to assess your audience allows you to see yourself from their perspective. And you need emotional awareness when dealing with direct reports as well as your manager. One of the most difficult duties of a manager or any leader is that they must be a filter. There are pressures on your boss that you cannot be privy to and they filter those pressures and demands so you are not affected. There are decisions that your manager has to make that you cannot know about due to confidentiality. So you only see a small part of what is happening in your manager's world. You need emotional awareness to support and make your manager look good, even when you do not fully understand all the factors behind their decisions.

Awhile back, I watched an interview with Martha Stewart. As most Americans know, Martha Stewart had some serious legal issues. But even with all the pressure she had been under, she showed very high emotional awareness in the interview.

One of Martha's close friends had written some very disparaging statements about her. When asked how she felt about her friend betraying her, Martha said that she obviously was not in contact with her previous friend. She was hurt, but she said, "I don't know why she wrote those things about me. I can't begin to judge her because I don't know what was going through her mind or happening in her life that might have caused her to do such a thing. I can only move forward." With that, the whole topic was finished.

Martha showed very high emotional awareness. She admitted the pain, but also had the ability to try and understand that her friend could have other issues going on in her life. Martha, picked herself up, brushed off the dirt, and kept moving forward.

A high degree of emotional awareness is needed for all successful leaders. Always weigh the impact of your words carefully and think how they may be misconstrued or misunderstood. Basically, it's the obvious, "Think before you speak."

Key #4 Communicate in the Positive

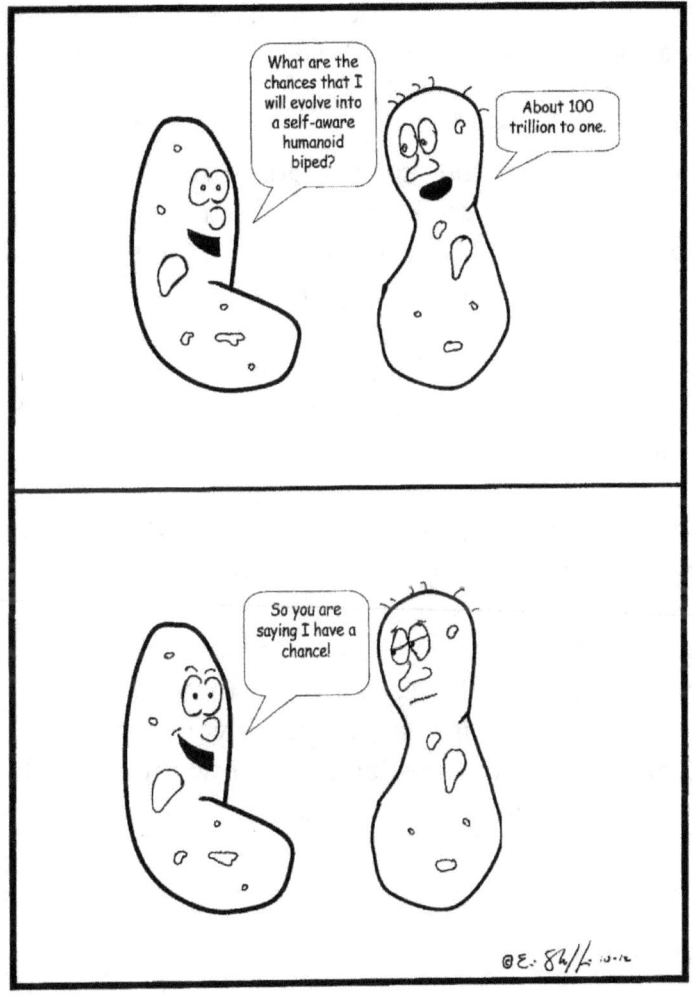

Being, thinking, and communicating in the positive take time and effort and are an absolute must for all leaders. Think about it. Who are the people that everyone wants to be friends with? The people who light up the room, who see the glass half full. These are positive people who do not talk about losses or disappointments, who find meaning and learning in setbacks. They are can-do people.

Imagine you are the captain leading your troops into a battle to overtake a beach. Your troops are on the landing craft protected by a metal bow that soon will lower as a ramp so they can storm the heavily fortified beach. As they get closer to the beach, they can hear the metallic ping of bullets. They can hear the cries of their comrades already in battle. In their chests, they can feel the percussive thud of explosions and they smell burning oil and sulfur. Many are nauseated from the smell and the constant undulations and spiked surges of the waves. They are petrified with fear knowing that at any moment, the ramp will drop and a hail of bullets will shower them with probable death. Do you think your troops would want to follow you if you are complaining about the dangers and whining about the difficulty and the probable lack of success?

In battle, a leader's pessimism, negativity, and lack of confidence and vision usually produce one result – death. But as powerful as the negative is, and even if there is an insurmountable amount of negative, a positive can defeat it all. A powerful and inspiring leader, who speaks using positive words and vision, can be the light that overtakes the entire negative. This positive leader can give his troops the strength to face and defeat the enemy on the beach.

The same can be said for leading your team in business. The business world is a battlefield, and your employees — your troops — are looking for you to guide and lead them to victory. No matter what adversity or obstacles they face, it is your job to be positive and inspire them to achieve success. It is your responsibility to build loyalty and vision to take your team to victory. If you show pessimism or weakness, it will infect your team like a virulent virus. A business leader's pessimism and negativity will have one result – demotivation and loss of great people.

To Be Human Is to Be Negative
For most people, talking in the positive is very difficult. In fact, a study done by Schrauf and Sanchez from Northwestern University found that the 'working emotion vocabulary' is typically weighted with words for negative emotions (50%) over positive (30%) and neutral (20%) emotions.

Inherently, the human psyche has the propensity to drift towards the negative. A March 2012 New York Times article reported that negative emotions require more thinking and so the information is more thoroughly processed than positive information. Roy F. Baumeister, a professor of social psychology at Florida State University, says that negative memories take longer to wear off and suggests it is an evolutionary factor writing, "Survival requires urgent attention to possible bad outcomes but less urgent with regard to good ones."

And this is not lost on those who work to shape public opinion about issues and people. An article in the Discovery News reported that 70% of the 2012 political advertisements were negative.

After the 2012 presidential debates, the news media was consumed with the "gotcha" moments. Moments of inconsistency, gaffs, or verbal slip-ups were chronicled and dissected by the media and pundits from both sides. It was fascinating that this was one of the rare election campaigns that the term "liar" was used to describe an opponent. In the past, terms such as distorted facts, inaccuracies, falsehoods, and the phrase "less than truthful" were used to describe an opponent's statements.

Several news programs commented that one wrong or negative statement by a candidate could mean the entire election. All of the positive attributes and good ideas of a candidate could be discounted by using a poor choice of words just one time.

Madonna under the Microscope
This holds true for many people in the public eye. I have seen most Super Bowl halftime shows since the mid-80s. Some of the shows were good and others great. I was curious to see what Madonna had in store for her recent halftime performance. I must admit the 12-minute show Madonna did was an excellent piece of work. In fact, I would have to say it was one of the better halftime shows I've watched.

The next day in the news there were cheers for her performance, but also a large amount of criticism and very negative comments. They called her old, a dinosaur, and irrelevant. Some said the performance was too gaudy and over the top. One critic said her voice was weak and she lip synched. Others said she was stiff like a board and lacked the agility of a 20-year-old.

What amazed me was the negative and destructive amount of comments from individuals that will never in their lives achieve 1/100th of Madonna's success. I asked myself, "How can so many be so critical? What about all the good things about her performance?" Some critics only focused on those minuscule items that otherwise may have gone completely unnoticed, dissecting them with a 10,000 power microscope and ignoring the totality of a great performance.

Test Your Positivity Skills
The first step to improving your presentations or communications is to recognize the negatives. This is not to say you will not use these words, but just be cognizant of them when you are speaking or writing.

Common negative prefixes include: a, an, anti, dis, in, il, im, ir, non, and un.

abandoned
abused
accused
addicted
afraid
aggravated
aggressive
alone
angry
anguish
annoyed
anxious
apprehensive
argumentative
artificial
ashamed
assaulted
at a loss
at risk
atrocious
attacked
avoided
awful
awkward
bad
badgered
baffled
banned
barren
beat
beaten down
belittled
berated
betrayed
bitched at
bitter
bizzare
blacklisted
blackmailed
blamed
bleak
blown away
blur

bored
boring
bossed-around
bothered
bothersome
bounded
boxed-in
broken
bruised
brushed-off
bugged
bullied
bummed
bummed out
burdened
burdensome
burned
burned-out
caged in
careless
chaotic
chased
cheated
cheated on
chicken
claustrophobic
clingy
closed
clueless
clumsy
coaxed
codependent
coerced
cold
cold-hearted
combative
commanded
compared
competitive
compulsive
conceited
concerned
condescended to

confined
conflicted
confronted
confused
conned

consumed
contemplative
contempt
contentious
controlled
convicted
cornered
corralled
cowardly
crabby
cramped
cranky
crap
crappy
crazy
creeped out
creepy
critical
criticized
cross
crowded
cruddy
crummy
crushed
cut-down
cut-off
cynical

damaged
damned
dangerous
dark
dazed
dead
deceived
deep
defamed
defeated
defective

defenseless
defensive
defiant
deficient
deflated
degraded
dehumanized
dejected
delicate
deluded
demanding
demeaned
demented
demoralized
demotivated
dependent
depleted
depraved
depressed
deprived
deserted
deserving of
pain/punishment
desolate
despair
despairing
desperate
despicable
despised
destroyed
destructive
detached
detest
detestable
detested
devalued
devastated
deviant
devoid
diagnosed
dictated to
different
difficult

directionless
dirty
disabled
disagreeable
disappointed
disappointing
disapproved of
disbelieved
discardable
discarded
disconnected
discontent
discouraged
discriminated
disdain
disdainful
disempowered
disenchanted
disgraced
disgruntled
disgust
disgusted
disheartened
dishonest
dishonorable
disillusioned
dislike
disliked
dismal
dismayed
disorganized
disoriented
disowned
displeased
disposable
disregarded
disrespected
dissatisfied
distant
distracted
distraught
distressed
disturbed
dizzy
dominated

doomed
double-crossed
doubted
doubtful
down
down and out
down in the dumps
downhearted
downtrodden
drained
dramatic
dread
dreadful
dreary
dropped
drunk
dry
dumb
dumped

edgy
egocentric
egotistic
egotistical
elusive
emancipated
emasculated
embarrassed
emotional
emotionless
emotionally bankrupt
empty
encumbered
endangered
enraged
enslaved
entangled
evaded
evasive
evicted
excessive
excluded
exhausted
exploited
exposed

fake
false
fear
fearful
fed up
flawed
forced
forgetful
forgettable
forgotten
fragile
freaked out
frightened
frigid
frustrated
furious

gloomy
glum
gothic
grey
grief
grim
gross
grossed-out
grotesque
grouchy
grounded
grumpy
guilt-tripped
guilty

harassed
hard
hard-hearted
harmed
hassled
hate
hateful
hatred
haunted
heartbroken

heartless
heavy-hearted
helpless
hesitant
hideous
hindered
hopeless
horrible
horrified
horror
hostile
hot-tempered
humiliated
hung up
hung over
hurried
hurt
hysterical

idiotic
ignorant
ignored
ill
ill-tempered
imbalanced
imposed-upon
impotent
imprisoned
impulsive
in the dumps
in the way
inactive
inadequate
incapable
incommunicative
incompetent
incompatible
incomplete
incorrect
indecisive
indifferent
indoctrinated
inebriated
ineffective

inefficient
inferior
infuriated
inhibited
inhumane
injured
injusticed
insane
insecure
insignificant
insincere
insufficient
insulted
intense
interrogated
interrupted
intimidated
intoxicated
invalidated
invisible
irrational
irritable
irritated

jaded
jealous
jerked around
joyless
judged

kept apart
kept away
kept in
kept out
kept quiet

labeled
laughable
laughed at
lazy
leaned on
lectured to
left out
let down
lied about

lied to
limited
little
lonely
lonesome
longing
lost
lousy
loveless
low

mad
made fun of
man handled
manipulated
masochistic
messed with
messed up
messy
miffed
miserable
misled
mistaken
mistreated
mistrusted
misunderstood
mixed-up
mocked
molested
moody
nagged
needy
negative
nervous
neurotic
nonconforming
numb
nuts
nutty

objectified
obligated
obsessed
obsessive
obstructed

odd
offended
on display
opposed
oppressed
over-controlled

over-protected
overwhelmed

pain
panic
paranoid
passive
pathetic
pessimistic
petrified
phony
picked on
plain
played with
pooped
poor
powerless
pre-judged
preached to
preoccupied
prejudiced
pressured
prosecuted
provoked
psychopathic
psychotic
pulled apart
pulled back
punished
pushed
put down
puzzled
quarrelsome
questioned
quiet

rage
rattled
regret
rejected

resented
resentful

responsible
retarded
revengeful
ridiculed
ridiculous
robbed
rotten
sad
sadistic
sarcastic
scared
scarred
screwed up
self-centered
self-conscious
self-destructive
selfish
sensitive
shouted at
shy
singled-out
slow
small
smothered
spiteful
stereotyped
strange
stressed
stretched
stuck
stupid
submissive
suffering
suffocated
suicidal
superficial
suppressed
suspicious

Just as important is to familiarize yourself with positive words and USE THEM! Turn the obstacle into an opportunity. Turn a mistake into a learning experience and so on. Here is a list of positive alternatives to the negative words.

A1
Absolutely
Absorbing
Abundance
Ace
Active
Admirable
Adore
Agree
Alert
Alive
Amazing
Appealing
Approval
Aroma
Attraction
Award
Bargain
Beaming
Beats
Beautiful
Best
Better
Bits
Boost
Bounce
Breakthrough
Breezy
Brief
Bright
Brilliant
Brimming
Buy
Care
Certain
Charming

Chic
Choice
Clean
Clear
Colorful
Comfy
Compliment
Confidence
Connoisseur
Cool
Courteous
Coy
Creamy
Crisp
Cuddly
Dazzling
Debonair
Delicate
Delicious
Delightful
Deluxe
Dependable
Desire
Diamond
Difference
Dimple
Discerning
Distinctive
Divine
Dreamy
Drool
Dynamic
Easy

Economy
Ecstatic
Effervescent
Efficient
Endless
Energy
Enhance
Enjoy
Enormous
Ensure
Enticing
Essence
Essential
Exactly
Excellent
Exceptional
Exciting
Exclusive
Exhilaration
Exotic
Expert
Exquisite
Extol
Extra
Eye-catching
Fair
Famous
Fantastic
Fascinating
Fashionable
Fast
Favorite
Fetching
Finesse

Finest
First
Fizz
Flair
Flattering
Flip
Flourishing
Foolproof
Forever
Fragrance
Free
Freshness
Friendly
Full
Fun
Galore
Generous
Genius
Gentle
Giggle
Glamorous
Glitter
Glorious
Glowing
Go-ahead
Golden
Goodness
Gorgeous
Graceful
Grand
Great
Guaranteed
Happy
Healthy
Heartwarming
Heavenly
Ideal
Immaculate

Impressive	Multi
Incredible	Natural
Inspire	Need
Instant	New
Interesting	Nice
Invigorating	Nutritious
Invincible	O.K.
Inviting	Opulent
Irresistible	Outlasts
Jewel	Outrageous
Joy	Outstanding
Juicy	Palate
K.O.	Palatial
Keenest	Pamper
Kind	Paradise
Kissable	Passionate
Know-how	Peak
Leads	Pearl
Legend	Perfect
Leisure	Pick-me-up
Light	Pleases
Lingering	Pleasure
Logical	Plenty
Longest	Plum
Lovely	Plump
Lucky	Plus
Luscious	Popular
Luxurious	Positive
Magic	Power
Magnifies it	Precious
Matchless	Prefer
Maxi	Prestige
Memorable	Priceless
Mighty	
Miracle	
Modern	
More	

Pride	Serene
Prime	Service
Prize	Sexy
Protection	Shapely
Proud	Share
Pure	Sheer
Quality	Shy
Quantity	Silent
Quenching	Silver
Quick	Simple
Quiet	Singular
Radiant	Sizzling
Ravishing	Skilful
Real	Slick
Reap	Smashing
Recommendation	Smiles
Refined	Smooth
Refreshing	Soft
Relax	Solar
Reliable	Sound
Renowned	Sparkling
Reputation	Special
Rest	Spectacular
Rewarding	Speed
Rich	Spice
Right	Spicy
Rosy	Splendid
Royal	Spotless
Safety	Spruce
Satisfaction	Star
Save	Strong
Scores	Stunning
Seductive	Stylish
Select	Subtle
Sensational	Success
Sensitive	Succulent
	Sun
	Superb

Superlative
Supersonic
Supreme
Sure
Sweet
Swell
Symphony
Tan
Tangy
Tasty
Tempting
Terrific
Thoroughbred
Thrilling
Thriving
Timeless
Tingle
Tiny
Top
Totally
Traditional
Transformation
Treasure
Treat
Trendy
Trust
Ultimate
Ultra
Unbeatable
Unblemished
Undeniably
Undoubtedly
Unique
Unquestionably
Unrivalled

Unsurpassed
V.I.P.
Valuable
Valued
Vanish
Varied
Versatile
Victor
Vigorous
Vintage
Vital
Vivacious
Warm
Wealth
Wee
Whiz
Whole
Whopper
Winner
Wise
Wonderful
Worthy
Wow!
Young
Youthful
Yule
Zap
Zeal
Zest
Zip

People want to follow positive leaders. They want a leader to take a negative situation and shine the light on the positive. One of the reasons John F. Kennedy and Ronald Reagan were so popular is they invigorated the positive. In tough times, they had a positive vision of future prosperity to energize the nation.

It is your job as a leader to invigorate and lead with a positive vision, attitude and communications. Your team listens to your every word and action; they are looking for you to show them the light at the end of the tunnel.

Key #5 Work for a Great Manager

"I hear you worked so many hours you passed out for 20 minutes. I just thought I'd make it clear that I'm not paying you for those 20 minutes."

I know, you are saying "No Kidding! Of course, I want to work for a great manager." Or perhaps you are saying, "I would like to work for a great manager, but there are only a few in my company."

For you to succeed, you have to be in the right situation. A manager with low emotional awareness or leadership capability will always drag you and your team down. You can only filter ill-conceived upper management decisions and direction for so long. A poor manager could lead you to emotional and career turmoil and possibly to a different company.

Many would say it is all about working for a great company. Every year there are lists of the best 100 companies to work for. I do agree that it's important to work for a company that rewards accomplishment, talent and commitment. However at the end of the day, it's your manager that you really work for. Gallup wrote in its survey findings, "People leave managers not companies...in the end, turnover is mostly a manager issue."

Gallup also showed that poorly managed work groups are 44 percent less profitable and on average 50 percent less productive than well-managed groups. Your manager needs to be a great coach and to champion your development so individual and organizational excellence, productivity and profits can be achieved.

Am I saying that if you are working for a less than adequate manager that you should quit your job? Absolutely not! What I am saying is that you need to plan your own development and growth. Look for those managers for whom you want to work. Plan your progression so that you can have the opportunity to work for and learn from the best your company has to offer.

You can work with a below average manager for a short period of time, and even learn what not to do as a manager. Even if you have disagreements with your current manager's leadership, it is vitally important that you are respectful and develop a strong relationship with your manager. Your job is to be an asset to your manager and company, understand the team and organizational goals and objectives. Your relationship with your manager is a two-way street so you help each other and the organization reach for a higher level of success.

So treat your manager respectfully and make a long term goal to move on to the next manager who is a role model and can teach and guide you. You are not only looking for a role model to learn from, but you are also making your political alliances. It is important to be politically aligned with the best in your organization.

Good managers/leaders want talented people on their teams. It is a win – win. You are offering your dedication and talent, and your manager guides and champions you while they benefit from your talents. If you are lucky you will find a coach and mentor in one boss. Someone who will act as an advisor or a sponsor and help you advance to the next level in your career.

Mary was one of my first managers and the best leader I've ever had the opportunity to work for. She was dedicated to developing her team and honing their strengths. In fact, when it came to teamwork, leadership, and unique ways to motivate, the top leaders of the organization imitated many of Mary's techniques and ideas.

Mary was the shining star of the organization and soon was promoted to Director then Executive Director. Even after Mary's promotions, she kept in contact with some on her previous team. I was one of the fortunate ones that Mary mentored. As I moved up the organizational career ladder, Mary was always available for advice and feedback and on two occasions was one of my sponsors when it came to promotional opportunities.

Identify the top leaders in your organization that you want to emulate, plan your pathway to work for these leaders, and if you're fortunate, you will find a leader like Mary to be a mentor and a sponsor.

"Vicious, intelligent and ruthless? Certainly. But I think my biggest asset is that I'm a survivor!"

Many would say that this should be Key #1. For much of my career, I would have agreed. One of the companies I worked for had an intense and long training period for managers. They beat it into our heads that hiring well must be the number one thing a manager/leader can do. Much of our training and role-plays were designed around hiring the best. Experience has taught me, however, that even if you hire the best, if you don't have and experience keys 1 through 5, you won't be able to keep your employees long.

There are books and matrices of hiring that can help you pick a good candidate. They can help you form the questions you may want to ask. Jack Welch's book, *Winning* gives an excellent outline of what to look for and evaluate. His 4-E and 1-P framework evaluates positive energy, energizing others, decision making, ability to execute and passion. And look for more than experience, look for future potential and talent.

Adam Bryant's book, *The Corner Office* is another excellent resource. He interviewed over 70 chief executives to gain an understanding of what it takes to lead and be a success.

In his book, he recognizes five key qualities:

1. Passionate Curiosity - relentless questioning that leads entrepreneurs to spot new

opportunities and helps managers understand the people who work for them, and how to get them to work together effectively.

2. Battle-Hardened Confidence – Confident perseverance in the face of adversity
3. Team Smarts – The ability to recognize the needs of the team and how to bring them together around a common goal.
4. A Simple Mind-Set – Be succinct and precise when presenting ideas. Get to the point.
5. Fearlessness – Be comfortable at being uncomfortable.

Simply put, the three questions you are trying to answer when hiring are:

1. Can they do the job?
2. Will they do the job?
3. Are they the right fit for your team?

In answering whether they can do the job, you want to understand their aptitude or ability to learn the position. This is probably the easiest to measure, as aptitude requirements are usually quantitative and concrete for technical aspects of a position. Do they have the experience or do they have the ability and talent to learn the position?

On the other hand, if you are trying to understand how effective they will be at a job, then you quickly go to the second question – will they do the job? This is going beyond the question of "can do" to trying to figure out what level of performance can be expected. Are they hungry, passionate, curious and fearless?

The "will" can be answered by high levels of past performance. Past performance is probably one of the best indicators of future performance. When you are evaluating past performance, ask for granular specifics, get into their thought pattern.

Why did they perform at a high level?

How did they do it?

What was their motivation?

Have them show you proof of their past performance. Have them bring in previous performance reviews.

Look for patterns, trends, motivators and values that led to their high performance. This is how to get to those qualities of passion, team smarts and fearlessness.

Top Performers Are Like Investments
There are some who think they can take an average performer and move them to the top. However, odds are, if they have only performed average in the past, they will probably perform the same for you. If you want a top performer, you will have to pay for them, and they will have volumes of proof with regards to their performance.

A top performer is like an investment that has a long history of paying high dividends. You want to see the proof of those previous dividends and you want the value of the high performer as part of your employee portfolio. Sure, there is always an exception to the rule. But why risk it?

Mediocre Performers Do Not Become Superstars
One of my close friends was a senior director for a large company. John had 11 managers and 130 representatives reporting to him. Whenever a representative was hired, John would conduct the final interview with the hiring manager to give the individual thumbs up or down. He took great pride in hiring the right managers and put a lot of trust in them to hire the right sales representatives.

On one occasion, John was conducting a final interview with a prospective candidate and the hiring manager. The candidate failed to impress my friend. The candidate's past performance was average. My friend pointed out the lack of performance to the hiring manager who was adamant that this candidate would perform and be one of his top representatives. He felt the candidate's past managers failed to fully understand her ability and that she was the right person for the job. John reluctantly approved the candidate's hiring.

A year later, I followed up with my friend to find out how the new hire was doing. He said, "Well, just as I expected. The new hire was mediocre."

I asked what he learned from the experience. He said he wouldn't be talked into a poor hire again and would make sure the hiring manager used more than his feelings to make an important hiring decision. I asked what the financial impact was of hiring the average individual. He said the difference between an average employee and a high performer was about $1 million annually in revenue.

Don't expect a mediocre performer to change to a superstar. Hire great employees and surround yourself with superstars so they can have a synergistic effect on your people and business. You could waste valuable time developing the average and you cost your organization millions in revenue. Spending a little more money on the best saves you time trying to move the average to the next level and it enhances your organization's revenue.

One or two occasions of high performance do not make a high performer. Every once in a while, a blind squirrel will find a nut. This is also true with performance – sometimes the low performers get lucky. They happen into a good situation, or take over a territory or market that was always high performing, or they have a partner or team that was responsible for most of the success.

You Can Feel a High Performer's Passion and Energy
High performers will have a long history of stellar performance. You can feel their passion and positive energy. They will be the individual that has a competitive spirit and a drive to succeed. They will be able to tell you stories sometimes all the way back to their childhood of how they tried to improve.

On one interview, I asked an applicant to tell me about her first job. She said she started working full time at 12 years old. She grew up in a poor family and needed to make money for school clothes. Her first summer job was 50 hours a week watching a baby and a toddler for a single mother. She was a babysitter until she was old enough to legally work at a fast food restaurant.

I asked her about her experience at the fast food restaurant and what she liked about the job. She said her managers tried to make the job fun by having a contest to see which employee had the most in their cash drawer. I asked her if there was a bonus associated with the contest. She said no, but it was the pride of winning and being number one for the most sales in her cash drawer. She always tried to be the winner, even when there was no contest; she was proud to have the most money in her register at the end of a shift. She was energetic, positive and had a can-do attitude.

So, did she show a desire to succeed? Was she hungry? Did she have drive and a competitive spirit? Did I want her on my team? Definitely!

Integrity, Drive and Success

Ron started off as an acquaintance, became a direct report, and over time, became a very close family friend. It was a few days before Christmas and my wife, son, and I were at the annual Christmas party thrown by Ron and his family.

I knew most of Ron's story. He grew up in Puerto Rico and came to the United States with his mother when he was a young man. We spent time talking about his past. Ron said when he was a young boy he didn't know he was poor until he went to school and noticed that all the other kids had shoes. He grew up eating beans and rarely had any meals with meat. It was usually only on special holidays that he would have a meal with chicken.

Ron knew he wanted to be something, but he couldn't succeed in the poverty that surrounded him in Puerto Rico. His chance came when one of his sisters married and moved to Youngstown, Ohio. She was pregnant with her first child and asked her mother to visit Youngstown and help for the first few months after the baby was born. Ron saw this as an opportunity to get to the States. He arrived in Youngstown with his mother and began his quest for success.

Ron could not speak any English, but he was able to find odd jobs to make enough money so that he could enroll at Youngstown State University. He said he had to work as often as he could to pay for school, his clothes and food, but he was determined to make the most of his education with good grades. He said the most difficult hurdle to overcome was that he had to teach himself English while he was in college.

He told me a funny story about his first English writing class. He had no idea what the professor was saying or what he was supposed to do for class. Ron noticed a pretty young girl in his class that seemed to be friendly. He knew he needed help to understand English and the homework assignments and he thought maybe this nice girl could give him a little help.

So Ron and a friend waited outside on the steps of the building where he had the English class. When he saw the girl, he pointed her out, allowing his English-speaking friend to approach her. The friend explained that Ron could not speak English, and asked if she would help as a translator to explain the homework and assignments for the class. She agreed to help Ron, and that was how he was able to successfully pass his first college English class. Ron eventually graduated from Youngstown State with a degree in chemistry.

In this example, Ron demonstrated integrity, honesty, drive, optimism and the pursuit of excellence. Now, after hearing this story, would you want to hire Ron? I can tell you his life story continued to be about integrity, drive and success. I can also say when he reported to me, he was one of the best sales representatives I ever had the pleasure of working with.

Oh, and the pretty girl who helped him with his English class? She is now his wife. They have two beautiful children, and because of Ron's tenacity, work ethic and passion, they are living the American Dream.

The Great Motivators for Success
I recently had dinner with a good friend and we discussed the internal motivator that makes someone a success. We narrowed it down to two primary factors:

1. The fear of failure
2. The intense desire to succeed

My friend asked which one was the greater motivator for success? I told him I wasn't sure. I would happily hire an employee who had either or both. He replied, "Precisely."

The Right Fit for You and Your Team

Just as it is important to have self and emotional awareness, it is important to have team awareness. To decide whether a prospective candidate is the right fit for you and your team, you must know your team and their strengths and weaknesses. What is the SWOT — Strengths, Weaknesses, Opportunities, and Threats — for your team? Where do you need improvement? Does the new candidate fit into that vacant spot that is needed to make your team complete? Are they a team player and would adding this person to your team provide synergy?

Building a team is like building your stock portfolio. You want a synergism of stocks on the upside with the right mix to protect the portfolio on the downside. If you are building a team, you want the diversity of team members to support the positive and decrease the effects of a negative.

A small organization was getting ready for a significant expansion in middle and upper level management. The organization hired an outside consulting firm to help them identify the talent that would be needed to fill the new roles.

The consultant met with the top leaders of the organization to gain insight into their needs and their expectations for the new leaders. One of the items the consultant asked about was diversity. The organization leaders let the consultant know they had a very well defined process and governance around diversity.

The consultant said that was not the kind of diversity he meant. He told them he was talking about the diversity of thought, personality and leadership styles. He encouraged the current senior leadership to take the **Myers-Briggs** Type Indicator (MBTI).

As a refresher, the MBTI preferences indicate the differences in people based on the following:

- How they focus their attention or get their energy (extraversion or introversion)

- How they perceive or take in information (sensing or intuition)

- How they prefer to make decisions (thinking or feeling)

- How they orient themselves to the external world (judgment or perception)

When the senior leadership got their results back they were amazed that they all scored as ENTJs.

They understood what the consultant was alluding to with regards to diversity. They realized they needed more than just the ENTJ representation in management and more diversity in thinking styles, personality and so on.

Diverse Team Thinking Creates Synergy
It is valuable to have diversity of thought on your team. This leads to synergy. Your team should not all have the same strengths, talents and personality traits. Think of the different roles each individual plays on your team. What role needs to be filled? How will the new candidate fill that role?

Part of team fit also revolves around a person's manageability and coachability. How does the individual want to be managed or coached? How have they interacted with their managers in the past? What have their managers said about them? Are they team players or lone wolfs?

I know some managers that would say, "I don't care if they are hard to manage, I just want performance." They say that until the hard-to-manage employee starts to affect the rest of their team. A great example of a hard-to-manage employee would be Terrell Owens. No one would argue that he is an incredible football player. But according to many news accounts, his coaches found him difficult to manage and he was a potential source of team angst and negativity. Team after team hired him because of his great talent, but he never stayed long with one team. A high performer can yield great results for themselves, but if they lack teamwork and manageability, they quickly become the one rotten apple that spoils the whole barrel.

Organizations are always trying to figure out the right mix for that perfect employee who will take the company to the next level. Companies try to find the answer by polling or questioning their top performers to find out what secrets they may have that are eluding everyone else. What is it that they do differently?

The Real Secrets to Success

One of my good friends, Pam, was a superstar representative. She started out 23 years ago selling copiers and was a top salesperson. She then moved to the pharmaceutical industry as a representative and — consistently over 15 years — was the top or one of the top sales representatives. No matter how her sales area changed or how the products changed, Pam was always number one. Predictably, Pam was always approached by the company and her managers to find out what her secret was.

One day we were at a national meeting, and Pam, as expected, was one of the top sales reps in the nation. And once again, senior leadership as well as a multitude of middle managers asked her repeatedly what her secret was. What did she say to her customers that caused her sales to be at such high levels? She had a secret and everyone wanted to know the answer.

She told me over coffee, "I couldn't tell them anything they wanted to hear. They wanted to know my sales pitch and I told them I was selling the features and benefits of our products. I find out what the customer needs by asking probing questions, and I identify how our products meet those needs." Then she unknowingly said the magic words of her success. "I work! I get up in the morning, get out of bed, and go to work! I see my customers and I don't get home until 6 pm. I do my job! Can't anyone figure that out?" It was as if her words were followed by the sounds of a thousand angels singing. The secret was good old-fashioned hard work and doing your best every single day.

Is that everything that contributed to Pam's success? No, of course there was more. I originally was hired to take over her territory after she had been promoted. She worked with me for two months to teach me and orientate me to her old territory. Pam had something different. I didn't know what the words were or the technical definitions were to what she had. I just knew she was different than anyone else I ever worked with.

Years later I understood that Pam took emotional intelligence to a new level. She understood her customers and dealt with them as people with feelings and needs. She was kind, friendly, trustworthy, and honest. Her sincerity was evident to all and she could connect with anyone. She could take the biggest idiot and turn them into a kitty cat. She could walk into a room of negative comments and turn them around to positive. She was naturally emotionally intelligent.

Now, here's some great news. People can be coached to enhance their emotional intelligence. My advice is to teach hiring managers and all leaders how to elevate their emotional intelligence and develop better skills. If a hiring manager is not trained in emotional intelligence, it may be difficult for them to identify those with high levels of it.

Pam also had four other secrets that added to the mystical formula to her success:

1. She was committed and dedicated to her job and had a strong work ethic.
2. She had an intense drive to succeed and do her best every day.
3. She was manageable and coachable. She wanted to learn and was eager to try new ideas.

4. She was a team player – Pam took pride in mentoring and teaching others. She was able to understand the team and the needs of the team and her boss.

Employees like Pam are not expendable. They are the 20% that can outperform the 80%. They are the ones you promote, and when you hire them, they do not come cheap. You pay for them, because they are your best investment. They are the stock or bond with a history of stellar performance and an expectation of continued performance. A good goal is to take your team from 20% of people like Pam to 30 or 40%.

Key #7 Surround Yourself with Smart People

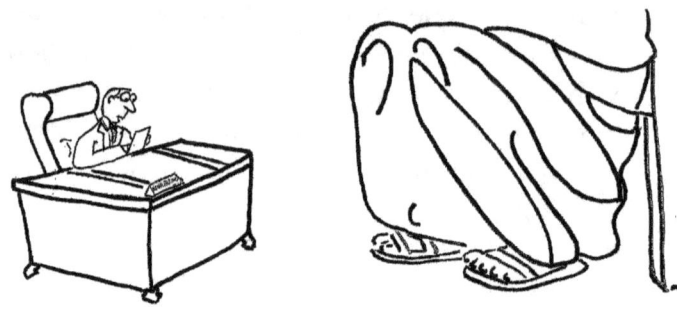

Omnipotent, All-Knowing, yes those are good attributes, but we are looking for a people person. Can you give me an example of a time you had to influence someone?

Show me your friends and I will show your future. You are the average of your five closest friends. I am not sure who came up with those quotes, but they are relevant when it comes to your teams and your professional acquaintances and actually life in general. I suppose you could say show me your direct reports and I will show you your future, or your performance is the average of your direct reports.

Surround yourself with the best people you can find, delegate authority, and don't interfere as long as the policy you've decided upon is being carried out.
~ Ronald Regan

President John F. Kennedy presented NASA and the nation with a historic challenge: to put a man on the moon and return him safely to Earth before the end of the 1960s. Kennedy set the vision, but left the' how' to the experts.

This kind of leadership shows true confidence. Micro managers and know-it-alls need not apply. This also goes back to diversification. Having a leader who thinks they have all the answers and requires that all decisions and actions go through them breaks the fundamental rule of leadership. A micro manager know-it-all will risk burning themselves out, stressing their teams, and making poor business decisions, which can lead to the collapse of companies which had great potential.

A great leader will always do what is best for the people, company and the stockholders. Whenever there is a difficult issue, hiring question or problem, great leaders always make the decision that is the best for the organization.

Surround yourself with the smart, the talented, the best, and you will elevate your team, their performance, and you will be doing what is right for the company and building long term success.

We all have times where we lose our cool. We all have friends, family, and employees who frustrate us or push our buttons. We are human beings and humans have emotions. Leaders and managers are often passionate about the company they work for and their teams. Leaders and managers are generally competitive and expect performance to be at very high levels. Sometimes that passion spills over into frustration and sometimes anger. It is not uncommon to have these feelings and they are to be expected.

Friends and family usually forgive and forget an emotional outburst, but an employee will always remember it.

Here are three simple guidelines to follow regarding becoming upset in the workplace.

1. Never leave a voicemail or email in anger. Always wait a few hours or even a day before writing the email or leaving the voicemail. In some cases, it may be advisable to have a colleague, friend, or coach review the communication.
2. Don't insult or yell at an employee or co-worker. Yelling may work for a high school football coach, but it generally does not go over to well in a professional organization.

3. Apologize, not just for losing your temper, but also when you make a mistake that negatively affects others. Saying you are sorry goes a long way and does not suggest weakness. It shows humility and courage.

Ah, yes, The mighty Achilles. I have heard of you and your men's bravery protecting my kingdom. I have decided to switch things up a bit and have my friend Rupract get some experience leading your men. You can take his old job of treasurer. Think of it as an opportunity to enhance your math skills.

No one would argue that Shaquille O'Neal is an amazing basketball player and that he was a force to be reckoned with on the court, except when he was at the free-throw line shooting foul shots. I guess you could say that was his weakness.

He struggled with his free-throws throughout his career and had a career average or 52.7%. He spent many hours trying to improve, but some would say all the practice never really helped. I wonder what would have happened if he took most of the time he spent on trying to improve his weakness to enhancing his strengths. How many more MVP awards would he have earned?

Naturally, if a weakness interferes with performance or a leadership competency it needs to be developed to get to the next level. However, if a weakness does not interfere with superior performance, why waste time trying to improve it?

I believe the best book written on this subject is *First Break All the Rules* by Marcus Buckingham and Curt Coffman. The book's recurring theme is to focus on your direct reports' strengths. Stop trying to fix a weakness that does not get in the way of their overall performance.

Bill George's book, *True North*, is another excellent leadership book. Bill comments that brilliance comes from exploiting strengths. He noted that some of the most extraordinary people in history, such as Margaret Thatcher and Gandhi had striking weaknesses, but through exploiting their strengths, were able to achieve amazing results.

Jim was the leader of a $120 million division that covered the most important and geographic area for the organization. He was the first leader to uncover the true business complexities of the area and built a team of top talent to manage the difficult business climate. Jim's division was one of the most profitable and fastest growing in the organization.

The CEO and president of the organization liked to hold weekly calls. Topics of the calls were often impromptu and randomly discussed subjects or new strategies that may improve business.

Jim was one of those individuals that made his decisions methodically and required research and deliberation before making strategic decisions. He was not a person who would make decisions on the fly or come up with quick solutions. Putting Jim on a conference call and expecting him to make quick remarks and input was not his strength.

Every two weeks, Jim would have an hour call with the president. He would give him an overview of his business, but the president never seemed interested in what was going well for Jim's division. Instead, he spent most of his time discussing Jim's being too slow to speak up on the weekly conference calls.

At the next weekly company call, Jim increased his participation, but it was not enough. He was again admonished by the president for not speaking up enough. And now, according to the president, the CEO was also commenting on Jim's lack of participation. They had a vision of what leaders do and wanted all their direct reports to fit the mold. They were ignoring Jim's real strengths. Not long after, Jim decided to leave the organization and went to work for the competition. The incident was not the only reason for his departure, but was an additive event.

Key # 10 Data Talks – Assumptions Walk

"Thanks for all your input Branston, but I've decided to go with my intuition."

Most of you reading this have probably heard of Lean Six Sigma, but in case you haven't, it is simply a methodology of improving or designing processes based on measurable data and facts. There are five steps to improving a process.

1. Define your problem: The definition is extremely important; it must be specific and precise. The questions are:
   a. What is the problem?
   b. When did it start?
   c. Who owns it?
   d. What is the goal and objective? Specific, Measurable, Achievable, Realistic, and Timely.
   e. What are the financial benefits if improved?
   f. Who are the customers of the problem?
   g. What are the customer's expectations?

2. Measure the problem: Without data to measure, you cannot fix a problem. The problem must be measurable.

3. Analyze the data: Based on the data, where is the root of the problem?

4. Improve the problem: Using a team of experts on the problem, develop measurable solutions and then test pilot the solution and assess the data for a 95% confidence of statistical improvement. Data must tell you if the improvement is the solution.

5. Control the improvement: Put standard operating procedures (SOPs) in place to make sure the improvement stays in place. Too many times, a problem is solved with a new improvement but people go back to their old ways and the improvement is negated.

Assumptions Can Cost Millions

Every project or problem or visionary improvement I have tackled with the Lean Six Sigma process started off with an assumption of what the answer was. Either the process owner, project team or I had an assumption—and 90% of the time we were wrong.

What I learned from working on multiple improvement projects is that solution-jumping without data can produce the wrong business decisions. These decisions can cost millions in opportunity for growth.

I am not discounting gut instinct; instinct is good to read between the lines to identify that maybe there is more to a story than meets the eyes, but it must be coupled with data and facts. A visionary idea is great, but to take it to reality it must be specific, actionable, factual and measurable.

Anytime you hear the words *I think* or *my feeling is,* assess if there is data to back up the statement. If the theory or idea sounds good, then look for the data to support or refute the idea before it becomes a decision.

This is not to say that a gut decision solution will not work. It's just that there could be a better more profitable decision. I have seen what is called the "decision-making shotgun." This is where a team loosely follows data and facts and makes decisions based on their gut feelings. They try a lot of different ideas hoping that one will work. The only problem is, if one does work, they don't know which one it is so they can't repeat it. This is also a very costly way to make decisions, and too much of this kind of decision making leads to decision mania.

Leaders do not make decisions based on a feeling or a gut reaction. Ronald Reagan said, "Trust, but verify." In other words, if your direct reports give a proposal for new company direction or campaign, trust the direct report, but verify that what they are proposing is accurate. The verification is done with data and facts.

Key #11 Get Rid of Waste

© John McPherson/Distributed by Universal Uclick via CartoonStock.com 2-25

Stupid Boss, Case No. 17: To avoid wasteful faxes,
Jim required all employees to fill out Fax Request
Forms and kept the fax machine in his desk.

To be an effective leader it is important to weed out the waste and focus on those activities that really matter. Waste is the destroyer of time, company profits and your energy.

What is waste? Waste is anything that:
- Does not add customer value
- The customer is not willing to pay for
- Does not add to the net benefit
- Sits
- Is stored
- Is overproduced
- Is reworked

In essence, if there is activity that does not add net value and meet customer expectations for quality and timeliness, then it is waste. In its purest form, business would eliminate all waste and focus just on meeting customer specifications and needs. This in turn, would lead to a positive net benefit.

A new vice president was concerned that one of the main products was under performing. He had a theory it was related to the marketing campaign. It was old and he wondered if it could be refreshed. He asked the marketing director to take a look at the campaign and make the necessary changes.

The director of marketing assigned a young marketing manager to work on the product campaign. The young manager feverishly worked to develop a new promotional campaign. Once it was completed he reviewed the new campaign with the director. The director asked the manager if he had done research to understand the campaign's expected effectiveness and if there was a means of measurement.

The director was disappointed to find out the manager did not completely investigate the potential effectiveness of the campaign and there were no plans to measure the results. The director asked the manager to reassess the campaign and develop a measurement system, as launching the campaign to an entire sales force could potentially be a waste of the time for the company, sales reps, and customers.

Waste is like throwing a pebble in a pond. The splash may be small but it has a ripple effect that spreads for yards. Waste has a way of spreading and infiltrating business. Sometimes waste can take precedence over good business practices. The waste can get so bad that an organization spends more time at waste then they do at business.

Simple ways to identify waste:

1. Does the activity meet a customer requirement? If your customer was in the meeting room with you or on the manufacturing floor with you, would they want to pay for the meeting, activity or procedure? If your answer is not an immediate yes, then it is probably waste.

2. Does the activity add value? Does it make your company money? Does it increase the net value of your company? If the answer is no, then it is probably waste.

3. Do you find yourself on conference calls but working on other items not pertaining to the conference call? If the answer is yes, then the conference call is probably waste. On the other hand, if you are working on other items during a conference call, and the call is not waste then the other activities you are doing is waste.

4. Do you have a lot of paperwork or emails that have been sitting on your desk or in your inbox for more than a week? If they are important, they should be dealt with first; if they can be put off, then they are waste. What would happen if they did not get acted upon? Would inaction change the company income? Or do you spend your time on the items that are not important only to put off the important revenue generating activities?

Waste is a revenue killer and customer turnoff. Eliminate what the customer does not want and does not want to pay for and focus on the revenue generating activities.

Key #12 Get to the Point

For a few years, I ran a team for a company owned by venture capitalists. I was required to make presentations to the CEO, CFO and president of the company. My manager at the time, who had worked for Bain and other consulting organizations, educated me in the proper way to communicate with the leaders of the organization.

As you move up the ranks in leadership, you will find yourself communicating in bullet points. You will not have much time to absorb the details, but you will need to know the big picture. Your presentations will need to follow a continuum. Middle managers usually want more detail, but as you move higher up the corporate ladder, your presentations should also elevate to a higher level. In other words, give the executive team a high-level overview of the subject. They are generally looking for your executive summary of a subject followed by bullet-pointed data to back up your summary. Be specific and to the point. If they ask questions, have the detail or information available for them to see.

When I was a new inexperienced sales representative, I dutifully listened to the sales trainers. I was taught that every time I met with a customer, I had to verbalize a lengthy two-sentence "core message" or main selling points of the product. I was also given a glossy sales aid to follow and was taught to use a pen to point to the features and benefits in a lengthy and rehearsed laborious one way communicative effort. I was very obedient and did exactly what I was trained to do. Long story short – my out-pouring of information about my products did not go over very well with my customers. In fact, by doing exactly what I was trained to do, one customer asked me to leave and never come back.

It wasn't long before my manager observed my intense spewing of product features and benefits at my customers. After a couple of customer visits, she calmly sat me down and informed me I had a severe case of "abdominal feature and benefit distress," which caused me to verbally spew words all over my customers that meant nothing to them. What I wasn't taught in training, she informed me, is that selling is not telling. She said many new sales professionals have the same affliction and not to be disappointed in myself. She said it was common for new sales reps to say too much without listening to what the client wanted.

Feature and benefit distress is not limited to sales calls, it can also happen when a presenter treats a PowerPoint presentation as a high school teenager would treat an essay. They put every bit of information on a page so they can capture all the credit. Putting paragraphs on a slide and presenting from that slide is torture to the audience and it exposes a presenter's lack of focus and confidence.

I have observed presenters trying to bury a problem or issue among the words of a slide. That way they can say, "Well, I told senior management that there was a problem." They think that making a slide full of words will save them.

When you are presenting to senior executives, middle managers and entry level executives it is important to be clear concise and to give them the amount of details they need. And as discussed in Key #4, communicate in the positive and be a solution provider.

Key #13 Be a Salesman

"THEY TESTED SOME BRAIN BOOSTING PILLS ON ME
AND NOW I'M SELLING MAPS. WANT TO BUY ONE?"

Think back to some of your favorite managers and
leaders. What was it about them that made them
your favorites? Was it how they were motivational
or their excitement and their passion for the
business and their teams? Was it the way they
explained their vision for the organization? After
you worked with them, did you feel a drive to
succeed? Did you want to become better and
improve your skill sets?

How does a great leader get so many followers? They are dynamic, positive, passionate, visionary, inspiring and know the needs of their teams. So if you add those qualities together what you get is the foundations for a great sales presentation.

A good example would be someone running for political office. They identify themselves with constituents, tell them the features (vision) about what they want to accomplish and how their plan will benefit them.

Next time you are watching TV observe how the commercials are set up. A commercial will usually start off explaining a problem. For example, flu symptoms. The commercial starts off with a person having a cough, stuffy nose, congestion and sleeplessness--the problem. Then the commercial explains how the medicine being pitched will quickly decrease the irritating symptoms-- the feature. Then finally the commercial will show the person breathing clearly and sleeping soundly-- the benefit.

A very simple sales process I define as the "6 P's of Persuasion" can be used or modified for leadership or coaching:

1. Prepare - Do your homework. What are your audience's needs and objections? What is their pain? How can you relieve the pain? What are their motivations?

2. Probe – Clarify to further understand the needs or concerns of your direct reports, teams or audiences.

   "I observe, gentlemen, that when I would lead you on a new venture you no longer follow me with your old spirit. I have asked you to meet me that we may come to a decision together: are we, upon my advice, to go forward, or, upon yours, to turn back?" ~Alexander the Great

   Understanding your team's concerns and objections has been a part of superior leadership as far back as recorded history. I sometimes wonder if it was a recognized attribute of leadership or if leaders at the time just realized the obviousness of understanding those they meant to lead.

3. Problem Solve – Resolve the objections by acknowledging, questioning and providing or eliciting ideas to solve them.

4. Pitch & Influence - Identify the features of what makes the idea great. Then relay how the features will benefit the team or audience.

5. Petition – Ask your team or audience for a call to action. You don't get unless you ask.

6. Post Evaluation - What did you do well? What could have been improved? What and who do you need to follow up with?

Earlier in the book I used the analogy of you being a military leader taking your team into battle. It is relevant to relate the competitive business environment to a battlefield. You are the leader that inspires your team to outperform the competition. To be effective, you need to influence, sell your vision and reason why your team works for your organization and why the direction they are going is the right one. You also need to understand there are hurdles and objections. Understanding the objections and difficulties and looking to your team for answers to those issues further solidifies their commitment to you and your organization.

Putting It All Together

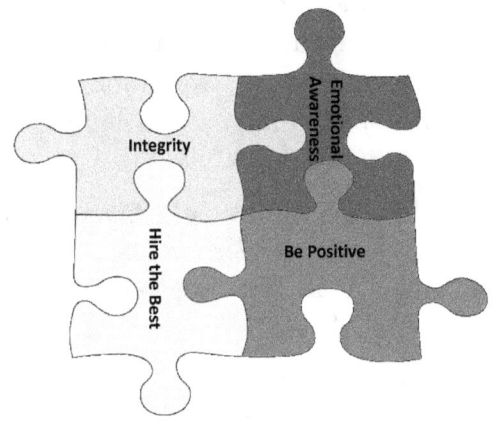

Now it is time to pull it all together. Taking those individual keys or puzzle pieces and putting them together to become an outstanding leader is a never ending journey to excellence. The final and most important key to leadership is your willingness to learn, grow and expand your skills. The final and most important key to successful leadership is YOU! But I bet you already knew that because the answer is obvious.

Works Cited

1. Schrauf, Robert W. and Sanchez, Julia (2004). The Preponderance of Negative
2. Emotion Words in the Emotion Lexicon: A Cross-generational and Cross-linguistic
3. Study. *Journal of Multilingual and Multicultural Development*. 25(2&3), 266-284.

4. Myers, Isabel Briggs with Peter B. Myers (1980, 1995). *Gifts Differing: Understanding Personality Type*. Mountain View, CA: Davies-Black Publishing. pp. 85–88.

5. Myers, Isabel Briggs; Mary H. McCaulley (1985) (in English). *Manual: A Guide to the Development and Use of the Myers-Briggs Type Indicator* (2nd edition ed.). Palo Alto, CA: Consulting Psychologist Press. pp. 52.

6. *There are Age-Related Changes I Neural Connectivity during the Encoding of Positive, but Not Negative Information,"* Cortex, May 2009

7. *The New York Times* Business Day (March 23, 2012) Praise Is Fleeting, but Brickbats We Recall

8. Discovery News (May 16, 2012). Why Do Negative Political Ads Work? Emily Sohn, retrieved from Discovery.com

9. *'Who Said You Could Wear My Sweater?'* Adolescent Siblings' Conflicts and Associations

with Relationship Quality," Child Development, March/April 2010

10. *"Weekends, Work, and Well-Being*: Psychological Need Satisfactions
and Day of the Week Effects on Mood, Vitality, and Physical Symptoms," *Journal of Social and Clinical Psychology*, January 2010

11. *An Empirical Study of Nigerian Entrepreneurs: Success, Motivations, Problems, and Stress*, By Chu, Hung M.; Kara, Orhan; Benzing, Cynthia Academic journal article from International Journal of Business Research, Vol. 8, No. 2

12. *"Extreme College Drinking and Alcohol-Related Injury Risk,"* Alcoholism: Clinical and Experimental Research, September 2009

13. Urban Titan (May 13, 2010). 10 Most Inspirational Speeches in History. James Massoud retrieved from Urbantitan.com

14. *The New York Times* Business Day (April 16, 2011) Distilling the Wisdom of C.E.O.'s. Adam Bryant

Suggested Reading

1. Jack Welch with Suzy Welch (2005). *Winning*. Published by Harpers Business pp. 81–90.

2. Bill George with Peter Sims (2007). *True North*. Published by Jossey-Bass pp. 109-115.

www.ingramcontent.com/pod-product-compliance
Lightning Source LLC
Chambersburg PA
CBHW072039190526
45165CB00018B/1177